Asian Indian AMERICANS

SPIRIT
of America®

Asian Indian AMERICANS

By Jean Kinney Williams

Content Adviser: K. V. Rao, Associate Professor of Sociology,
Bowling Green State University

The Child's World®
Chanhassen, Minnesota

8

Asian Indian AMERICANS

Published in the United States of America by The Child's World®
PO Box 326 • Chanhassen, MN 55317-0326 • 800-599-READ • www.childsworld.com

Acknowledgments
The Child's World®: Mary Berendes, Publishing Director

For Editorial Directions, Inc.: E. Russell Primm, Editorial Director; Sarah E. De Capua and Pam Rosenberg, Line Editors; Elizabeth K. Martin, Assistant Editor; Olivia Nellums, Editorial Assistant; Susan Hindman, Copy Editor; Joanne Mattern, Proofreader; Matthew Messbarger, Ann Grau Duvall, and Deborah Grahame, Fact Checkers; Tim Griffin/IndexServ, Indexer; Cian Loughlin O'Day, Photo Researcher; Linda S. Koutris, Photo Selector

Photos
Cover/frontispiece: Oregon Historical Society

Cover photographs ©: David Young-Wolff/PhotoEdit

Interior photographs ©: AFP/Corbis: 11, 17, 18, 22; Catherine Karnow/Corbis: 20, 24-bottom; Corbis: 7 (Janez Skok), 8 (Richard A. Cooke), 10 (Earl & Nazima Kowall), 13 (Gunter Max Photography), 16 (David H. Wells), 21 (David G. Houser), 23, 24-top (Nik Wheeler), 25-top (Reuters NewMedia Inc.), 28 (Ted Spiegel); Getty Images: 6 (Ami Vitale), 27 (David McNew); Getty Images/ Hulton Archive: 25-bottom; Getty Images/Time Life/Ed Clark: 15; Hulton-Deutsch Collection/Corbis: 9, 19.

Registration
The Child's World®, Spirit of America®, and their associated logos are the sole property and registered trademarks of The Child's World®.

Library of Congress Cataloging-in-Publication Data
Williams, Jean Kinney.
  Asian Indian Americans / by Jean Kinney Williams.
    p. cm. — (Our cultural heritage)
  "Spirit of America."
  Includes bibliographical references (p.) and index.
  Contents: Life in India—Adjusting to a new land—Indian Americans today—Influencing American culture.
  ISBN 1-59296-015-4 (lib. bdg. : alk. paper)
  1. East Indian Americans—Juvenile literature. [1. East Indian Americans.] I. Title. II. Series.
  E184.E2W55 2004
  973'.04914—dc21
                              2003004288

13   16   22

Contents

Chapter ONE

Life in India

Delhi, India, is one of the largest cities in the world.

INDIA IS THE SECOND MOST POPULATED country in the world. Located south of China—the world's most populated country—it is a land of contrasts. To the north are snowcapped mountains, while to the west is desert. Fertile farmlands can be found in the central region. Fourteen languages are recognized by the government, among the hundreds of languages spoken by its 1 billion people. While most Indians live in small villages, India also has some of the world's biggest cities. Mumbai (which used to be called Bombay), Delhi, and Kolkata (which used to be called Calcutta) have more than 10 million people each.

Most of India's people practice the Hindu religion. Some are Muslim. Still others are Buddhists, Sikhs, Christians, and Jains. Hinduism is among the world's oldest religions. It dates back to about 6000 B.C. Hindus believe in a Supreme Being, or God. However, God takes many forms. For example, the god Vishnu rewards good and punishes evil. Many Hindus are strict **vegetarians.**

The god Shiva is one of the main gods of the Hindu religion.

The first known civilization in India began about 2500 B.C. in the northwest's Indus River Valley. There were two large cities called Harappa and Mohenjo-Daro. In 1500 B.C., fierce Aryans swooped down from Asia and ruled in the north.

The Mauryan Empire began about 325 B.C. and also ruled northern India. A few hundred years later, the Gupta Empire began. It lasted from A.D. 320 to about 500. That

India's many temples include the Ellora Caves (above). These ancient temples were carved from cliffs in western India more than 1,000 years ago.

era is called India's Golden Age. **Literature,** art, mathematics, and philosophy reached great heights under the Guptas. Many Hindu temples were built during this time.

Muslim armies invaded India during the next thousand years. The most notable Muslim rulers were from the Mughal Empire, which began about 1525. Many important landmarks, such as the Taj Mahal in Agra, were built under the Mughals.

At about the same time, Europeans became interested in India's tea, spices, silks, and other resources. Great Britain's East India Trading Company ruled much of India for more than 200 years. Then in the mid-1800s, the British government took control of most of India.

In 1885, the Indian National Congress was formed to gain independence from the British. In 1920, it was led by Mohandas Gandhi, who loved his fellow Indians and

8

hated violence. Gandhi led Indians in nonviolent protests against the British. Indians **boycotted** British products and refused to pay taxes.

Meanwhile, India's Muslims wanted their own country. In 1946, rioting broke out between Indian Hindus and Muslims. During the next several years, nearly 500,000 Indians died in the riots. When Great Britain granted India independence in 1947, it also created the country of Pakistan. (Eastern Pakistan became the independent country of Bangladesh in 1971.) The majority of people in Pakistan are Muslim. Today, tension remains between the Hindus of India and Muslims of Pakistan.

Mohandas Gandhi (center) was an important Indian leader in the fight for independence from Great Britain.

As an independent nation, India has become one the fastest-developing countries in the world. Its universities train many scientists and engineers. It exports (or sells to other countries) cotton, tea, chemicals, and electronics. India also has a huge movie industry. It is the largest **democracy** in the world.

Many people in India live in poverty and are so hungry they will sort through garbage to look for food.

India faces many challenges, however. Millions of Indians live in poverty. Cities are polluted and overcrowded. While India provides the world with Nobel Prize-winning scientists, more than 300 million Indians are illiterate, which means they cannot read or write. Government inefficiency and complicated laws make running a business difficult.

As a result, many Indians who want a better life for themselves and their children have left the country permanently. They have moved to Australia, New Zealand, Great Britain, and other places. Most, however, have come to the United States. There are nearly 2 million Asian Indians living in America. They have made many contributions to American culture and society. Today, Asian Indian Americans are valued employees in companies across the United States. Some own their own companies. But, like many immigrants to America, their success has not come without struggle.

PEACE BETWEEN INDIANS AND PAKISTANIS IN THEIR PART OF THE WORLD STILL seems far away. One source of conflict is a region called Kashmir. Both countries claim it. But some Indians and Pakistanis are trying to help the peace process from the United States.

Many young people grow up in India learning that Pakistanis are enemies. But in the United States, they are often happy to meet someone from their part of the world, even a Pakistani.

Pakistani students from the University of Minnesota organized a peace concert that featured a Pakistani rock band called Junoon. One Pakistani student wanted to start the concert by playing both the Indian and the Pakistani national anthems. But too many Pakistanis protested, and the "Star Spangled Banner" was played instead. Another recent peace concert took place in New York. There, organizers encouraged Indians and Pakistanis to celebrate one thing they have in common—gaining independence from Great Britain in 1947.

The organizers of these events and many other young people hope that the second generation of Asian Indian and Pakistani Americans in the United States can help make peace happen in their parents' homelands.

11

Chapter TWO

Adjusting to a New Land

AT THE CHICAGO WORLD'S FAIR IN 1893, MANY curious Americans were interested in learning about Hinduism from India's Swami (or priest) Vivekanada. But in most places in the United States, Indians weren't welcomed. No Asians were.

The first Asian Indians came to America in the early 1900s after arriving in Vancouver, on Canada's west coast. They slowly moved south to work for the railroads or lumber mills in Washington and Oregon. At first, Americans saw Asian Indians as strange. Their religion, clothing, and customs were unfamiliar. As a result, they were sometimes treated badly and denied jobs.

In spite of bad treatment and immigration laws that strictly limited the number of

12

Asians allowed into the country, some people still left India to settle in the United States. One Asian Indian group, the Sikhs, became farmers in central California. Wealthier Asian Indians sent their children to the United States to attend American universities. The United States allowed those who were college educated or successful businessmen (there were few female Asian-Indian immigrants) to enter the country, too. Many of those Asian Indians planned to work for India's independence away from the British government's watchful eyes.

By the 1940s, there were a few thousand well-educated Asian Indians living in America. They began asking the U.S. government to give Asian Indians more rights. In 1946, they were allowed to become citizens.

Some Asian Indian Americans practice the Sikh religion and worship in temples such as this one.

▸ The American
Institute of Indian
Studies was established
in 1961 by a group of
American scholars who
were interested in
Indian culture. Head-
quartered in Chicago,
the organization is
today a leading resource
for Indian studies in the
United States.

That was especially helpful to Asian-Indian
farmers in California, who hadn't been
allowed to buy land.

Still, fewer than 7,000 Asian Indians
immigrated to America in the next 18 years.
They began arriving in larger numbers after
1965. That year, Congress passed the
Immigration and Nationality Act, allowing
many more Asian Indians into the country.

The Immigration and Nationality Act
changed the patterns of Asian Indian immigration to the United States. Before 1965,
few women came to America. Many immigrants were farmers or students. These early
immigrants settled mainly in the Pacific
Coast states. After 1965, the number of male
and female immigrants became about the
same. Farmers and students were joined by
doctors, engineers, and scientists. These new
immigrants began making their homes all
across America.

With each passing decade, America's
Asian Indian population increased greatly. In
1970, there were about 75,000 Asian Indians
in America. By 2000, there were almost 2
million. Who are these new Americans?

14

ASIAN INDIAN AMERICANS are successful in many areas of American life. One has even been elected to the U.S. Congress.

Dalip Singh Saund was born in Punjab, India, in 1899. He arrived in California in 1920 to study. Although he earned a doctorate degree, he became a farmer to earn a living. He continued his studies and enjoyed public speaking. He married an American woman and in 1949 became an American citizen. After he was elected to be a judge in Westmoreland, California, he decided to run for Congress in 1956.

It was a close race, but Saund won the election. In 1962, he suffered a stroke, which ended his political career. Since then, no Asian Indian American has followed him to Congress—yet.

15

Chapter THREE

Asian Indian Americans Today

Asian American Indian children are expected to do well in school.

ASIAN INDIAN AMERICANS are one of the best-educated **ethnic** groups in America. Their children are expected to do well in school. The parents often remind their children that with an education, they can be successful in life. One of the most successful Asian Indian Americans is Pavam Nigam. An immigrant to the United States, he earned his fortune in the computer software business.

In fact, America's Asian Indian immigrants are at home in the world of computers.

16

About 300,000 Asian Indian Americans work in California's Silicon Valley, the heart of the computer industry. Some of the computer world's biggest success stories feature Asian Indian Americans.

Vinod Dham was a top engineer in developing the Pentium processor for computers. Today, the best computers feature Pentium processors. At age 27, Vinod Khosla and four employees began his company, called Sun Microsystems. By the late 1990s, it was worth billions of dollars. Sabur Bhatia had an idea for free e-mail that people could access from anywhere. He sold his finished product, Hotmail, for $400 million.

Sabeer Bhatia is one of the people who created the Internet e-mail service known as Hotmail.

There are many Asian Indian American success stories in science and research, too. Narinder Kapany discovered fiber optics in 1955. Three Asian Indian Americans have

Kalpana Chawla was an Asian Indian American astronaut and the first Indian-born woman to fly into space.

won the Nobel Prize: Har Gobind Khorana in 1968 for his work in medicine, Subramanyan Chandrasekhan in 1983 for physics, and Amartya Sen in 1998 for economics.

As a girl growing up in Karnal, India, Kalpana Chawla dreamed of going into space. She came to the United States to study aeronautical engineering. She later became an American citizen. In 1994, she was one of only 20 people selected to join NASA's astronaut program. Three years later, Chawla became the first woman born in India to fly into space. Dr. Chawla was a crew member on the space shuttle *Columbia* when it broke apart during its return to Earth on February 1, 2003.

Perhaps you've seen advertisements for the Bose radio or stereo. Asian Indian American Amar Bose created a superior speaker system

that is popular in car and home stereos. Bose was born in 1930 in Philadelphia. His father was an Asian Indian immigrant.

Not all Asian-Indian immigrants have been scientists and students. During the days of British rule, Asian Indians spread out to other British-ruled countries, including some in Africa. In the 1970s, some of those African nations rebelled against foreign rule. There was much fighting. Many Asian Indians living in those countries left and came to America. They weren't as

Under British rule, many Asian Indians, such as these Asian Indian troops in Egypt, lived in other British-controlled countries.

educated as earlier Asian-Indian immigrants. However, they arrived ready to work and often found jobs in hotels. Today, many of America's small hotels and motels are owned by Asian-Indian Americans. Many big-city taxicab drivers are Asian Indians, too. They have also influenced American music, movies, exercise, food, and more.

Some Asian Indian Americans work as taxicab drivers in big cities.

WHILE ASIAN INDIAN AMERICANS HAVE EXPLORED ALL AREAS OF AMERICAN life, many stay faithful to their Indian roots. For example, Asian Indian American Hindus no longer have to hold religious services in each others' homes as they might have in the 1960s. Today, Hindu temples can be found across the United States, from California to Connecticut. American temples often imitate the architecture of temples in India. They are important cultural centers where American Hindus pray together and continue to learn about their religious roots.

Chapter FOUR

Influencing American Culture

Manoj Night Shymalan is a successful Asian Indian American filmmaker.

MANOJ NIGHT SHYAMALAN IS A SECOND-generation Asian Indian American. This means he was born in America to parents from India. His parents are medical doctors. When Shyamalan was growing up, he said he always was expected to be the top student in his class. He knew his parents wanted him to be a doctor, too. They weren't pleased with his decision to study

filmmaking in college. When his movie script for *The Sixth Sense* (which he also directed) was a huge hit, his parents knew that he had chosen the right career.

Asian Indian Americans are also musicians, authors, and restaurant owners. They and their cultural **heritage** are a part of everyday American life.

Have you heard of yoga? It's a popular form of exercise that began in India hundreds of years ago. Yoga poses combine stretching and strength with **meditation.** Many people find that yoga challenges them physically and relaxes them.

For Americans who like to stay healthy, Indian food is a good choice. Jagdev "Jesse" Singh immigrated to America from northwest India and now owns a

Yoga, a form of exercise that began in India hundreds of years ago, is practiced by many people in the United States.

A meal of popular Asian Indian American foods

An Asian Indian American mother and her son at an Indian restaurant in Washington, D.C

restaurant in Ohio. He says Americans like the Indian food on his menu because much of it is low in fat, and he offers many vegetarian dishes.

Asian Indian curry is a popular dish in America. There are many kinds of curry. One of the curries is made from chopped onions and tomatoes cooked in oil with many spices such as garlic and ginger. Add chicken to it, and you have chicken curry. Americans sometimes mistakenly expect Indian food to be very spicy. Singh said that Indian cooks use many spices in their food, but not always hot spices.

Deepak Chopra is an Asian Indian American doctor. He believes that meditation, instead of medicine, is often a better way to stay healthy. Chopra has written best-selling books suggesting ways for people to improve their health.

The unique sounds of the sitar, an Asian Indian stringed musical instrument, are sometimes heard in American pop music. Sitar player Ravi Shankar first brought Eastern and Western music together in the 1960s. He was named Musician of the

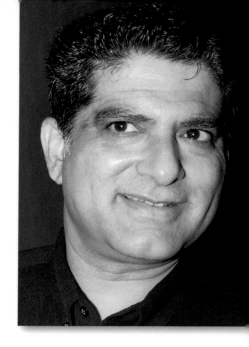

Asian Indian American Deepak Chopra is a best-selling author.

Ravi Shankar is a famous Asian Indian musician who plays the sitar.

Year by *Billboard* magazine in 1967. Shankar inspired rock superstars such as the Beatles. In 2003, Shankar's daughter Norah Jones won an amazing eight Grammy Awards, including Best New Artist, for her first album *Come Away with Me.*

Asian Indian American Zubin Mehta is a superstar in the world of classical music. He directed the New York Philharmonic Orchestra and has conducted orchestras around the world.

Zubin Mehta has conducted orchestras around the world.

Movies from India are popular with Asian Indian Americans, even if they were born in America. There are many Asian Indian movie theaters across the United States.

Some young Asian Indian Americans are willing to allow their parents to arrange marriage for them. In this way, they follow an Asian Indian tradition that is hundreds of years old. Asian Indian American newspapers, such as *India Abroad,* feature advertisements from parents looking for a future son-in-law or daughter-in-law.

Asian Indian Americans have made a big impression on their adopted country. As a

Asian Indian Americans joined all Americans in mourning the deaths of those killed in the September 11, 2001, terrorist attacks.

Interesting Fact

▶ Sanskrit is the ancient language of India. Yoga poses, even in U.S. classes, are often referred to by their Sanskrit names.

▶ Ved Mehta was born in India and lost his sight as a young boy. He came to the United States to attend an Arkansas school for the blind. He then continued his education at Yale and Oxford. He became a U.S. citizen in 1975 and went on to become an editor at *The New Yorker* magazine. He has also written a number of books, including a biography of Mohandas Gandhi, that have been translated into at least eleven languages.

reporter named Sarita Sarvete wrote, "We Indians have more in common with Americans than most Americans realize. We are just as individualistic, outspoken, **diverse,** and **multi-cultural** as Americans." America is richer for their contributions.

An Asian Indian American woman performs a traditional Hindu dance.

2500 B.C. First known civilization inhabits northwest India's Indus River Valley.

1500 B.C. The Aryans, from Asia, invade India.

500 B.C. The religion called Buddhism is founded in India.

320–500 A.D. The Gupta Empire begins its rule, resulting in India's "golden age."

1525 The Muslim Mughal Empire rules India; Europeans begin arriving at about the same time.

1600s The British East India Trading Company first visits India in 1608 and begins building factories; it slowly gains control of much of the country until the British government takes over India in the mid-1800s.

1947 India becomes an independent country; it also is split apart to form Pakistan.

1955 Narinder Kapany discovers fiber optics.

1956 Dalip Singh Saund is elected to the U.S. Congress.

1965 Congress passes a new law making immigration to the United States easier for Asian Indians.

1968 Har Gobind Khorana wins the Nobel Prize for his work in medicine.

1970 About 75,000 Asian Indian Americans live in the United States.

1983 Subramanyan Chandrasekhan wins the Nobel Prize for physics.

1997 Kalpana Chawla becomes the first woman born in India to fly in space.

1998 Amartya Sen wins the Nobel Prize for economics.

2000 The population of Asian Indian Americans grows to almost 2 million.

Glossary Terms

boycott (BOY-kot)
To boycott is to refuse to buy a product or use a service. To protest British rule, Indians boycotted British products and refused to pay taxes.

democracy (deh-MOK-ruh-see)
A democracy is a government made up of representatives chosen by its citizens. India is the largest democracy in the world.

diverse (dih-VURS)
People or events that are diverse differ from each another. Indians are just as individualistic and diverse as Americans.

ethnic (ETH-nik)
Ethnic refers to the traits that describe a certain race or group of people. Asian Indian Americans are one of the best-educated ethnic groups in America.

heritage (HAIR-ih-tij)
Heritage refers to the customs or culture of a group of people. Asian Indian Americans and their cultural heritage are a part of everyday American life.

literature (LIT-ur-ah-chur)
Literature is the part of a culture that is expressed through writing. Literature, art, mathematics, and philosophy reached great heights during India's Gupta Empire.

meditation (meh-dih-TAY-shuhn)
Meditation is to deeply focus one's thoughts on something. Yoga exercises combine stretching and strength with meditation.

multicultural (muhl-ti-KUHL-chuh-ruhl)
Something that is multicultural includes many different cultures or ethnic groups. Indians are as multicultural as Americans.

vegetarians (veh-juh-TAYR-ee-yunz)
Vegetarians' diet excludes meat; a person who eats no meat, except for fish, is called a vegetarian. Many Hindus are strict vegetarians.

For Further INFORMATION

Web Sites

Visit our homepage for lots of links about Asian Indian Americans:
http://www.childsworld.com/links.html

Note to Parents, Teachers, and Librarians:
We routinely verify our Web links to make sure they're safe,
active sites—so encourage your readers to check them out!

Books

Bandon, Alexandra. *Asian Indian Americans.* Parsippany, N.J.: Silver Burdett, 1995.

Gilmore, Rachna. *Lights for Gita.* Gardiner, Me.: Tillbury House, 1995.

Sreenivasan, Jyotsna. *Aruna's Journeys.* St. Louis, Mo.: Smooth Stone Press, 1997.

Vijayaraghavan, Vineet. *Motherland.* New York: Soho Press, 2002.

Places to Visit or Contact

Ganesh Temple
45-57 Bowne Street
Flushing, NY 11355
718/460-8484

Rama Temple
10915 Lemont Road
Lemont, IL 60439
630/972-0300

Index

About the Author

JEAN KINNEY WILLIAMS LIVES AND WRITES IN CINCINNATI, OHIO. Her nonfiction books for children include *Matthew Henson: Polar Adventurer* and a series of books about American religions, which include *The Amish, The Shakers, The Mormons, The Quakers,* and *The Christian Scientists.* She is also the author of *The Pony Express* and *African-Americans in the Colonies.*